SUPER SPORTS TEAMS

INSIDE THE
NEW ENGLAND
PATRIOTS

CHRISTINA HILL

Lerner Publications ◆ Minneapolis

SPORTS THRILLS
MEET
RESEARCH SKILLS

Lerner SPORTS

Free Database Trial: **lernersports.com**

Lerner Publications **Company**
An imprint of Lerner Publishing **Group**, Inc.
241 First Avenue North
Minneapolis, MN 55401 USA

For reading levels and more information, look up this title at www.lernerbooks.com.

Main body text set in **Aptifer** Slab **LT Pro** / **Typeface** provided by Linotype AG

Library of Congress Cataloging-in-Publication Data

Names: Hill, Christina, author.
Title: Inside the New England Patriots / Christina Hill.
Other titles: New England Patriots
Description: Minneapolis, MN : Lerner Publications , [2023] | Series: Super Sports Teams (Lerner Sports) | Includes bibliographical references and index. | Audience: Ages 7–11 years | Audience: Grades 2–3 | Summary: "Before Tom Brady joined the New England Patriots in 2000, the team had zero Super Bowl wins. When he left they had six. Learn about the team's history and Brady-less future"— Provided by publisher.
Identifiers: LCCN 2021055005 (print) | LCCN 2021055006 (ebook) | ISBN 9781728458083 (Library Binding) | ISBN 9781728463414 (Paperback) | ISBN 9781728462363 (eBook)
Subjects: LCSH: New England Patriots (Football team)—History—Juvenile literature. | Football—Massachusetts— History—Juvenile literature. | Super Bowl—History—Juvenile literature.
Classification: LCC GV956.N36 H55 2023 (print) | LCC GV956.N36 (ebook) | DDC 796.332/640974461—dc23/ eng/20220126

LC record available at https://lccn.loc.gov/2021055005
LC ebook record available at https://lccn.loc.gov/2021055006

Manufactured in the United States of America

TABLE OF CONTENTS

Kicker Stephen Gostkowski is the all-time leader in field goals for the New England Patriots.

THE GREATEST COMEBACK

FACTS AT A GLANCE

- From 1960 to 1970, the team was called the **BOSTON PATRIOTS**.

- The Patriots lead the National Football League (NFL) with 11 **SUPER BOWL** appearances.

- The greatest comeback in Super Bowl history was in 2017 when the **PATRIOTS** came back to win from 25 points behind.

- Former Patriots quarterback **TOM BRADY** tops the NFL charts with his seven Super Bowl wins.

The New England Patriots faced the Atlanta Falcons in the Super Bowl on February 5, 2017. This game is remembered as one of the greatest comebacks in NFL history. The first quarter was scoreless. But in the second quarter, the Falcons scored three touchdowns and took a 21-point lead. Patriots kicker Stephen Gostkowski made a field goal with two seconds left in the first half. The score was 21–3.

By the end of the third quarter, the Falcons were still in the lead with a score of 28–9. The lead seemed too large for the Patriots to come back and win. But they had star quarterback Tom Brady. He had already played in seven Super Bowls and knew he could turn the game around.

During the fourth quarter, Gostkowski made a 33-yard field goal for three points. With only 10 minutes left in the game, the Patriots were still trailing by 16 points. But then Brady threw a 6-yard pass to wide receiver Danny Amendola, who scored a touchdown. Patriots running back James White scored a two-point conversion. The Patriots were closing the gap. After another touchdown and two-point conversion, the game was tied 28–28.

For the first time in NFL history, the Super Bowl entered overtime. White scored a final touchdown, giving the Patriots an epic victory of 34–28. The win was their fifth Super Bowl title. What a comeback!

Danny Amendola (*left*) had eight catches for 78 yards and a touchdown in the 2017 Super Bowl.

James White (*right*) set a new Super Bowl record by scoring 20 points against the Falcons.

Tom Brady played 20 seasons for the Patriots under the leadership of team owner Robert Kraft.

THE PATS

When American pro football first started in the early 1900s, there were two leagues in the United States—the American Football League (AFL) and the NFL. Billy Sullivan Jr. was a Boston, Massachusetts, businessperson who wanted his city to have a pro football team. In 1959, he heard that the AFL needed an eighth team. So Sullivan jumped at the chance to become a team owner.

From left to right: Boston mayor Ray Flynn, Billy Sullivan Jr., and Massachusetts governor Michael Dukakis show their support for the Patriots as they head to their first-ever Super Bowl.

Sullivan ran a contest for people who lived in Boston to submit ideas for the team name. Patriots was chosen because Boston was a key city in the Revolutionary War (1775–1783). Fans call the team the Pats for short.

After choosing players, the team was almost ready to play football. The only thing missing was a home stadium. In 1960 and 1961, the Patriots played at Boston University Field. In 1962, they played at Harvard Stadium. From 1963 to 1969, the Patriots played at Fenway Park, the home field of the Boston Red Sox pro baseball team. In 1970, they were back at Harvard.

The Patriots played two seasons at Harvard Stadium.

The Patriots' mascot is a Revolutionary War soldier named Pat the Patriot. He was designed by a newspaper cartoonist in 1960.

On game days, Gillette Stadium is packed with fans.

Finally, in 1971, the Patriots found a home at Foxboro Stadium, 22 miles (35 km) south of Boston. Since the team was no longer playing in Boston, they changed their name to the New England Patriots. In 2002, workers tore down Foxboro and built a new stadium in the same place. Gillette Stadium can seat 65,878 football fans.

Patriots owner Robert Kraft also owns the New England Revolution soccer team.

Victor K. Kiam bought the team from Sullivan in 1988, but Kiam ran out of money and couldn't keep running the franchise. James Orthwein became the head owner in 1992. He wanted to build the franchise back up until he could find a permanent owner. Robert Kraft was a businessperson and a big Patriots fan. His lifelong dream came true when he bought the franchise from Orthwein in 1994.

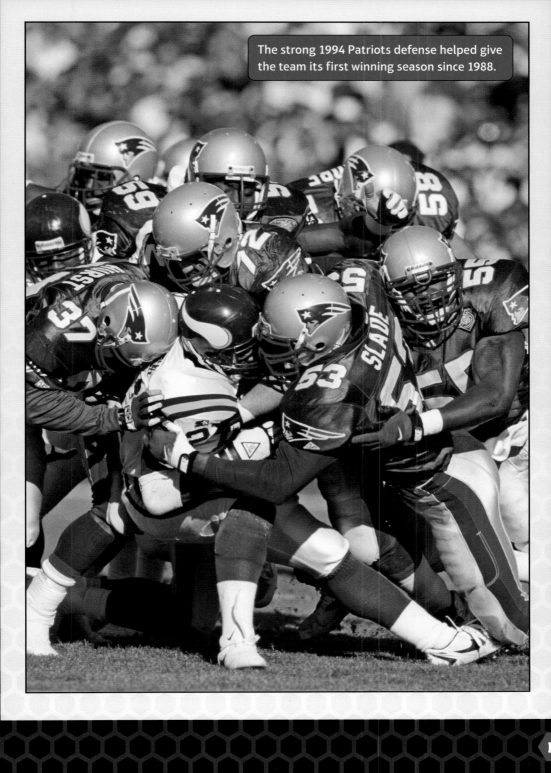

The strong 1994 Patriots defense helped give the team its first winning season since 1988.

Patriots defender Tedy Bruschi holds the 2002 Super Bowl trophy after the game.

AMAZING MOMENTS

The Patriots are known for their amazing moments on the football field, but it wasn't always easy. The team struggled to win games in their first few seasons. But in 1976, they had their best season yet with 11 wins. In 1986, the Patriots played in their first Super Bowl. But the Chicago Bears crushed them 46–10.

In 2000, things began to really turn around for the Patriots. Led by coach Bill Belichick and quarterback Tom Brady, the team won their first Super Bowl in 2002. They set an NFL record with 21 wins in a row from 2003 to 2004. Then they won the Super Bowl again in 2004 and 2005.

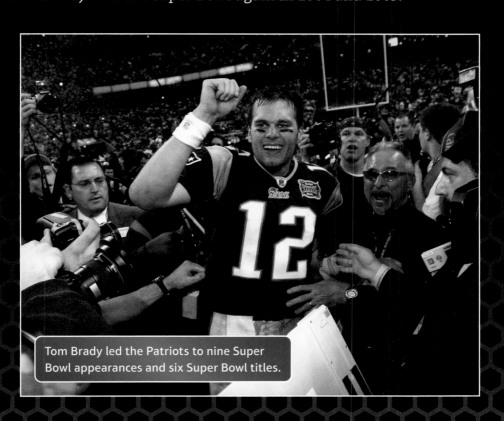

Tom Brady led the Patriots to nine Super Bowl appearances and six Super Bowl titles.

In 2007, the Patriots became the third team in NFL history to go undefeated for an entire regular season. They also set an NFL record at that time with 589 points. They entered their sixth Super Bowl with a 16–0 record, and most fans expected them to win. But New England's perfect record ended that night when the New York Giants scored a winning touchdown with only 35 seconds left. Despite that big upset, the Patriots marched on.

Patriots players celebrate a touchdown in 2007.

In 2015, the Patriots made their eighth Super Bowl appearance against the Seattle Seahawks. New England fans had waited 10 long years since their last Super Bowl victory. The game was close until the very end. Near the end of the fourth quarter, the Seahawks attempted to throw for a touchdown at New England's 1-yard line. Patriots defender Malcolm Butler intercepted the pass in an amazing play. The Patriots won the game 28–24, winning their fourth Super Bowl title.

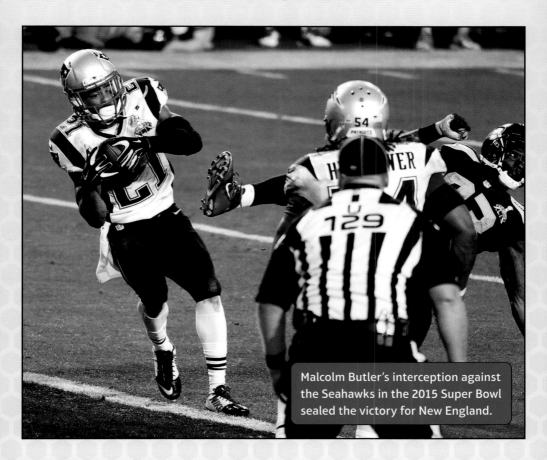

Malcolm Butler's interception against the Seahawks in the 2015 Super Bowl sealed the victory for New England.

Tom Brady is the most successful quarterback in NFL history.

PATRIOTS SUPERSTARS

Since the start of the team in 1960, the Patriots have had many star players. John "Hog" Hannah was one of the best offensive linemen in NFL history. He was known for his size and strength. Hannah played for the Patriots from 1973 to 1985. In 1978, he helped the Patriots set an NFL single-season record with 3,165 rushing yards. Hannah was the first Patriot to enter the Pro Football Hall of Fame.

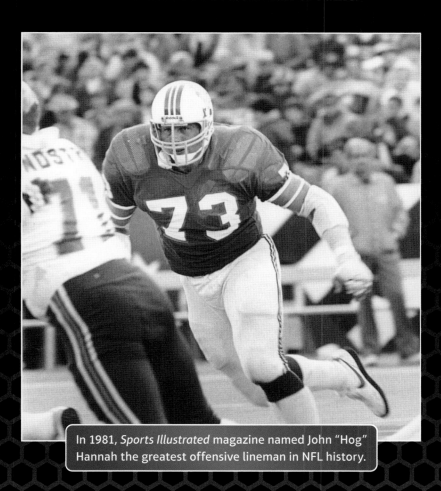

In 1981, *Sports Illustrated* magazine named John "Hog" Hannah the greatest offensive lineman in NFL history.

The Patriots drafted wide receiver Stanley Morgan in 1977. Morgan was superfast and averaged more than 20 yards per catch in his first five seasons. In 1986, he caught 84 passes for 1,491 yards and scored 10 touchdowns.

Drew Bledsoe was New England's starting quarterback from 1993 to 2001. He was the first overall pick in the 1993 draft and is the Patriots' second-highest passer of all time with 29,657 career yards and 2,544 completed passes.

The greatest superstar in the team's history is the record-shattering Tom Brady. He proved that hard work and patience pay off. Unlike Bledsoe, Brady was overlooked as a college player. Scouts thought he was not as strong or athletic as many other players.

In 1995, Drew Bledsoe was the youngest quarterback at the time to play in the Pro Bowl, the NFL's all-star game.

PATRIOTS FACT

Bill Belichick has led his team to six Super Bowl wins, two more than any other head coach in the NFL.

Bill Belichick has coached longer than any other current head coach in the NFL.

The Patriots selected Brady 199th overall in the 2000 NFL Draft. He got his big chance in his second season. He became the starting quarterback after Bledsoe was injured. Brady proved that the scouts were wrong about him, and he should have been selected much earlier in the draft. His success comes from being smart, focused, and calm on the field.

Brady became one of the greatest quarterbacks in NFL history. While playing for the Patriots, he earned 17 division titles and led his team to 13 conference championships. He also appeared in nine Super Bowls with New England and earned six Super Bowl titles.

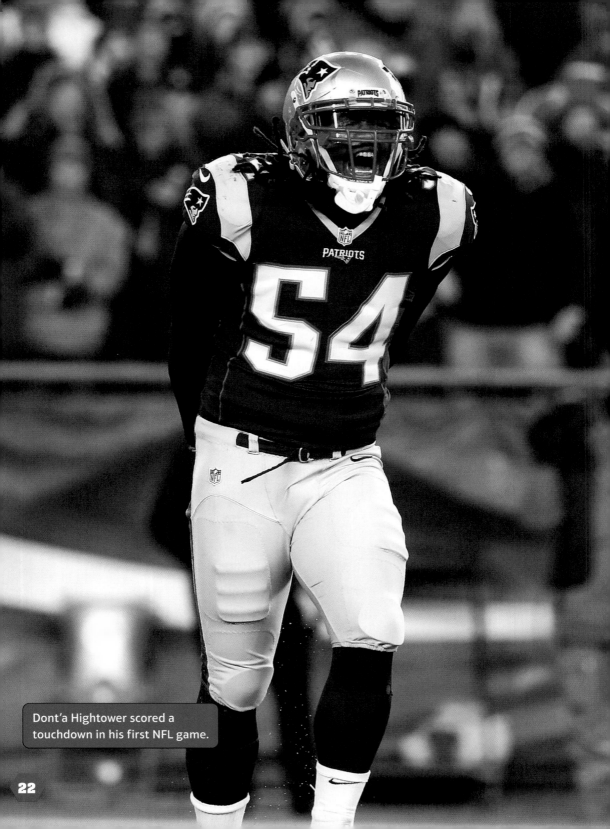

Dont'a Hightower scored a touchdown in his first NFL game.

The Patriots selected defender Dont'a Hightower in the first round of the 2012 NFL Draft. He helped his team win three Super Bowls. Hightower has been team captain three times and is part of the Patriots 2010 All-Decade Team.

Running back James White joined the Patriots in 2014. In the 2017 Super Bowl, White set a new record with 14 catches. He also set a record for scoring 20 points with two rushing touchdowns, one touchdown catch, and one two-point conversion. White is the first and only player in the NFL to score points in overtime during a Super Bowl.

James White is a member of the Patriots 2010 All-Decade Team.

In 2021, rookie quarterback Mac Jones was one of the most accurate passers in NFL history.

DO YOUR JOB

The Patriots claim that the secret to their continued success is the phrase "do your job." These three words are often printed on the team's hats, T-shirts, and other gear. The phrase is also on the side of one of their Super Bowl rings.

"Do your job" means that each player walks onto the football field ready and prepared to play hard, pay attention, and perform to the best of their ability. The words help to unite the players. Every athlete must play their part to help the whole team.

A Patriots fan displays a "do your job" sign to remind the team to focus on playing the game.

New England's success over the years has led to devoted and dedicated fans. The Patriots have sold out almost every game played at Gillette Stadium. In 2020, the Patriots were the second most popular team in the NFL.

The Patriots are embracing a new group of star players. Tom Brady left the team in 2020, which opened a spot for a new quarterback. Cam Newton took over for one year. But in 2021, the Patriots signed first-round draft pick Mac Jones. Jones instantly became the starting quarterback as a rookie. They also signed defender Matthew Judon, who played his first five seasons with the Baltimore Ravens. Tight end Hunter Henry joined the Patriots from the Los Angeles Chargers.

Anything is possible for the Patriots in the years to come. Coach Belichick is focusing on improving the team's defense and getting them back to the Super Bowl. Led by their experienced coach and their new quarterback, the Patriots have a bright future.

Matthew Judon (*center*) had 236 total tackles with the Baltimore Ravens before signing a four-year contract with the Patriots in 2021.

Hunter Henry scored his first touchdown for the Patriots in his fourth game with the team.

Wes Welker holds the Patriots' record for most catches in a season.

PATRIOTS
SEASON RECORD
HOLDERS

RUSHING TOUCHDOWNS

1. LeGarrette Blount, 18 (2016)
2. Curtis Martin, 14 (1995)
   Curtis Martin, 14 (1996)
3. Corey Dillon, 13 (2006)
   BenJarvus Green-Ellis, 13 (2010)

RECEIVING TOUCHDOWNS

1. Randy Moss, 23 (2007)
2. Rob Gronkowski, 17 (2011)
3. Randy Moss, 13 (2009)
4. Stanley Morgan, 12 (1979)
   Rob Gronkowski, 12 (2014)

PASSING YARDS

1. Tom Brady, 5,235 (2011)
2. Tom Brady, 4,827 (2012)
3. Tom Brady, 4,806 (2007)
4. Tom Brady, 4,770 (2015)
5. Tom Brady, 4,577 (2017)

RUSHING YARDS

1. Corey Dillon, 1,635 (2004)
2. Curtis Martin, 1,487 (1995)
3. Jim Nance, 1,458 (1966)
4. Stevan Ridley, 1,263 (2012)
5. Craig James 1,227 (1985)

PASS CATCHES

1. Wes Welker, 123 (2009)
2. Wes Welker, 122 (2011)
3. Wes Welker, 118 (2012)
4. Wes Welker, 112 (2007)
5. Wes Welker, 111 (2008)

SACKS

1. Andre Tippett, 18.5 (1984)
2. Andre Tippett, 16.5 (1985)
3. Andre Tippett, 12.5 (1987)
   Mike Vrabel, 12.5 (2007)
   Chandler Jones, 12.5 (2015)
   Matthew Judon, 12.5 (2021)

GLOSSARY

comeback: winning a game after being close to losing

conference: a group of sports teams that play against one another

draft: college players chosen to play on a professional sports team

field goal: three points scored when the football is kicked between the goalposts

franchise: a team that is a member of a pro sports league

offensive lineman: a player whose main job is to block defenders

pro: short for professional, taking part in an activity to make money

regular season: when all of the teams in a league play one another to determine playoff teams

rookie: a first-year player in a sport

two-point conversion: a football play made after scoring a touchdown; a team chooses to try to advance the ball across the goal line for two points instead of kicking the ball for one point

LEARN MORE

Christopher, Matt. *On the Field with Tom Brady.* New York: Little, Brown and Company, 2018.

Levit, Joe. *Meet Tom Brady.* Minneapolis: Lerner Publications, 2023.

The New England Patriots
https://www.patriots.com

The Patriots Hall of Fame
https://www.patriotshalloffame.com/hall-of-fame/

Scheff, Matt. *The Super Bowl: Football's Game of the Year.* Minneapolis: Lerner Publications, 2021.

Sports Illustrated Kids—Football
https://www.sikids.com/football

INDEX

PHOTO ACKNOWLEDGMENTS

Image credits: Bob Levey/Stringer/Getty Images, p.4; Ronald Martinez/Staff/Getty Images, p.6; Kevin C. Cox/Staff/Getty Images, p.7; Jim Rogash/Stringer/Getty Images, p.8; City of Boston Archives/Wikimedia, p.9; Nick Allen/Wikimedia, p.10; Rick Stewart/Stringer/Getty Images, p.11; Jim Rogash/Stringer/Getty Images, p.12; Simon Bruty/Staff/Getty Images, p.13; Ezra Shaw/Staff/Getty Images, p.14; Andy Lyons/Staff/Getty Images, p.15; Chris McGrath/Staff/Getty Images, p.16; Harry How/Staff/Getty Images, p.17; Billie Weiss/Stringer/Getty Images, p.18; Sporting News Archives/Icon SMI/Newscom, p.19; Jamie Squire/Staff/Getty Images, p.20; Kevork Djansezian/Stringer/Getty Images, p.21; Adam Glanzman/Stringer/Getty Images, p.22; Adam Glanzman/Stringer/Getty Images, p.23; Maddie Meyer/Staff/Getty Images, 24; Jevone Moore/Icon Sportswire/Newscom, p.25; Bob Levey/Stringer/Getty Images, p.26; Maddie Meyer/Staff/Getty Images, p.27 Jim Rogash/Stringer/Getty Images, p.28

Design element: Master3D/Shutterstock.com.

Cover image: Al Bello/Staff/Getty Images